Tropical Christmas

COLORING BOOK

JESSICA MAZURKIEWICZ

DOVER PUBLICATIONS, INC.
MINEOLA, NEW YORK

Sun replaces snow in this festive coloring book that celebrates Christmas in the tropics! Humorous illustrations rendered by popular artist Jessica Mazurkiewicz include sandcastles and palm trees bedecked with holiday lights and ornaments, snow ladies wearing bikinis, and various scenes featuring Santa Claus sporting sunglasses and a Hawaiian shirt! No reason to be cold at Christmas when you can spend it at the beach! These 31 pages of whimsical designs are perforated and unbacked and ready to be colored in your choice of media.

Copyright

Copyright © 2020 by Dover Publications, Inc.
All rights reserved.

Bibliographical Note

Tropical Christmas Coloring Book is a new work,
first published by Dover Publications, Inc., in 2020.

International Standard Book Number
ISBN-13: 978-0-486-84177-9
ISBN-10: 0-486-84177-4

Manufactured in the United States by LSC Communications
84177401
www.doverpublications.com
2 4 6 8 10 9 7 5 3 1
2020

CHRISTMAS IS BETTER AT THE BEACH!

Beachy
& Bright
Holiday Wishes!